love's highway

BY ARTHUR BRIGHTY

ISBN 13: 978-1-935986-86-7
First print edition, 2016
Published by Liberty Mountain Publishing. Printed in the U.S.A.

A DIVISION OF
LIBERTY UNIVERSITY

Liberty Mountain Publishing
Lynchburg, VA
www.LibertyMountainPublishing.com
You can contact Arthur Brighty at
arthurbrighty@gmail.com.

DEDICATION

I wish to dedicate this book to two very special
people with whom I have had the privilege of
sharing my life. First, my precious wife of 50
years has been a wonderful friend; she has kept
me stable and focused on the important things
in life, namely my walk with the Lord and our
family. Her intercession for me has been
invaluable, and I can truthfully say that I would
not be where I am today without her.

Secondly, I dedicate this to a person who is now
home with his Lord, my dear brother in Christ,
Patrick O'Leary. I only knew him for 15 years,
but the spiritual input he gave to me and my
family was amazing, and when he went home at
the age of 96, he left a legacy of spiritual nuggets
that are still blessing us to this day. We know he
is very happy now, but we still miss his joyous
presence and countenance.

ACKNOWLEDGMENTS

I wish to acknowledge Danny Megard and
Leland Caldwell for their practical help and
encouragement in establishing and formatting
this book, as well as John Blain for his knowledge
and encouragement from the very outset and
Eric Hyde for his imaginative book cover design.

And finally, Pastor Faw of Joy Church; this great
man of God has spiritually fed me in ways too
numerous to mention, his encouragement to me
over this book has been astounding and
absolutely invaluable.

I thank them all from the bottom of my heart.
Their input has been very precious to me.

God bless them.

FOREWORD

Love's Highway is a collection of poems that the Lord graciously allowed me the privilege of writing through the inspiration and quickening of the Holy Spirit. I believe them to be the heart of God revealed in a very simple but relevant, challenging, and profound way. It has given me — as well as everyone who reads them, I hope — an insight into God's heart from a new perspective. As I penned His thoughts, I was frequently moved by how He prompted me to reveal His feelings, often uncovering a truth that I had previously missed.

This whole experience has greatly altered and improved my own walk with the Lord, as my spiritual eyes have been opened very wide to the amazing LOVE that our Lord has for His creation.

LOVE'S POWER

Holy Spirit, Love's power to release
To the longing soul that yearns for peace
To answer heart's most deepest cry
With such love no one can buy
So Your power from deep within
Leads me to my heavenly King
Therein my soul is truly blessed
As I find Your perfect rest

HIGHER PLAIN

Holy Spirit, such love unfeigned
Lifts me to a higher plain
Where love's blessing, ever flows
Which Your abundant grace bestows

JESUS GAVE ALL

Jesus, my Lord, You bowed Your knee
When on that day in Gethsemane,
With tormented soul for what lay ahead,
You cried to the Father for what You did dread.
And though Your blood made it hard to see,
You gave Your will, and said, "Let it be."
Then many came with spear and sword
To take the Lamb, whom we adored.
He went before His false accusers
And suffered much by His abusers.
They mocked, reviled, and scorned my King
Then scourged His back, as they did bring
My Lord, My Friend, to that shameful tree
Where His nailed body hung for me.
Then pure love, racked with pain,
Gave up the Ghost but not in vain.
For from His side flowed the crimson flood

So all are cleansed, through His precious blood.
The price is paid, I am set free
Because my Jesus died for me.
Thank God, Thank God, Thank God for CALVARY!

HOLD FAST

When all seems lost in that hopeless place
I run to see the Master's face
And there I find the answers clear
As I've sought love and have drawn near
Love is the one who gives me sight
So I can trust for He is my right
Then onward as we go
To gain the victory over our foe
What blessed joy this walk does bring
As I hold fast to my heavenly King

LOVE QUICKENS

Spirit of love, You quicken me
As You draw me close to Thee.
As You lead me through the maze,
Opening my soul to Your loving gaze.
For Your love, my soul's desire,
Freed me from the pit of mire,
Cleansing me through love's precious blood,
Leading me in love's wondrous flood.

LAMB OF GOD

Lamb of God, eternal love
Fulfilled all righteousness to receive the dove.
Humbled Himself to endure temptation
And through obedience, secured salvation.

HEALING

Precious Lord, you made it clear
That Your healing is very dear
To Your heart and perfect will.
This causes us, with faith, to be still.
And as we look at the scars You bore
They show a love that's very pure.
And as our faith touched Your garment's hem,
Rivers of virtue no one could stem
Would touch our bodies and our souls
And then command us, "Be made whole!"
As Your heavenly balm takes hold,
We find a strength that makes us bold.
With healing in Your wings
You raise us up to higher things.
So we with you do walk in health
Having received our heavenly wealth.

GOD'S LOVE

God of love, You are our stay
And as You lead us in Your way,
We are strengthened with a threefold cord
So we may be in one accord.
Then as we go, we're Your delight
For through Your Son we are made light.
And with Your light to shine the way
We can be sure we'll never stray.

———————— ⚮ ————————

THE TABLE

Father, You've prepared a table
Where we do dine and are made able.
You fill our cup to overflow
As we go forth, in light's pure glow.

LOVE'S TENDER TOUCH

Spirit of Love, Your tender touch
Meets me—my need—oh, so much.
Your love descends to my deepest blight
Then lifts me up in Your glorious light.
Because Your love has such potential
(A proven truth that's most essential)
On my knees, to You I pray
Your gentle love exerts its sway.

UNFAILING LOVE

God of love You never fail
As Your pure love hung on a nail
Such wondrous love I can't conceive
But through Your love I do believe

LOVE'S DOOR

Spirit of love, to the cross You draw
As the Son of love opens wide the door
Through the love I boldly walk
And then conform to Your heavenly talk.
Tender love does lead us in
To where we get so cleansed from sin.
There is no better place to rest
Than in love's bosom, mightily blessed.

———————— ✿ ————————

STRONG LOVE

Spirit of love, so strong and pure
Renews my mind and makes it sure,
Directs my steps that I may walk
And keep my tongue from foolish talk.

BLOOD

So as You hung, heart fully broken,
Your love poured out, a heavenly token
To show mankind the depth and measure
And heavenly wonder of Your divine treasure.
Also, with grace and mercy, flowed
Your amazing light; it freely glowed,
It reached the darkest, deepest pit
Exposing dross wherever it lit
Then purged our souls with Your precious blood
Giving us victory through the flood.

———————— ⚬ ————————

SWEET LOVE

God of love, what sweet refrain
Rings from the heaven of Your domain.
Such love, so pure it melts my heart.
From it, I won't, I can't, depart.

AMAZING LOVE

God of love, Your blood did run
So freely out of Your dear Son.
To contemplate this amazing grace
Causes me to fall upon my face.

LIVING WATERS

Living waters from Your throne do flow
To the souls of the ones You know.
They wash and cleanse our mortal beings
And bring new live and new beginnings.
These rivers of life do far extend
Beyond ourselves to meet new friends.
And with the spirit of love to guide,
So leads them in. And to abide
Into the arms of Jesus, they fall.
Then He becomes their all in all

KNEE DRILL

Father, as we storm Your court
With our prayers so deeply sought,
You give assurance that You hear
When on our knees, we do draw near.
Then You calm our anxious hearts
As Your solace You impart.
You then restore expectancy
To the soul that yearns for Thee.
In this, we joyfully receive
All our hearts do conceive,
Releasing peace sublime
As we rest in sweet recline.

OUR NEED

Dear Lord I come, racked with emotion,
Into Your presence with great compulsion
Where You command me, to take heed
And to overcome with Your good seed.
It is the truth that sets me free
So I would gain all You have for me

I'M ADOPTED

Thank You, Lord, for choosing me,
Making me part of Your family.
You accepted me, just as I stood,
Then shared Your love, as only You could.
Such love adopted this prodigal soul
Giving me a home, making me whole.
And then Your seal You did endow
As I'm filled with glorious power.

GOD'S SECRET PLACE

In Your secret place we dwell
Free from fear, knowing all is well.
You still our minds, encourage hope,
Then show us how we should cope.
With tender love and compassion there,
Our hearts rejoice, for You do care.
Grace and mercy abound through love
As we receive all from above.

THE TABLE

What joy! What joy! Your words I taste
For at Your table, there is no waste.
Your precious bread we consume
Before our journey we resume.
And as we tread that narrow road
We won't forget our final abode.
For at the supper, we shall meet
Our loving Saviour and be complete.

RESURRECTION LIFE

They laid His body in a tomb
A borrowed grave, where there was room.
Across its mouth, they did place
The stone they thought would hold God's grace.
But the angels had another mission;
They rolled it back, without permission.
And Grace walked out — it was God's plan
To bring a glorious truth to man.
It is such joy to know God's heart,
For the resurrection life He does impart
Brings peace and truth we can embrace.
And when we see our Lord's dear face,
See the scars that caused such pain,
Our worship, Lord, nought will restrain.
And through all eternity, we'll bring
Never-ceasing praises to our heavenly King.

IT IS FINISHED

The battle raged, the fight was on
For three long hours, righting the wrong.
With steadfast faith in the Father's touch
Even hell itself could not so much
As stop true love, advancing through
Preaching to all who He foreknew.
We know pure love is not diminished
For we heard Him say, "It is finished."

FREE

When I run to the Father's side
I find a place I can reside
Free from all life's fears and woes
Amazing grace, the Lord bestows
Then I can rest in His embrace
Having fears removed, without a trace.

EMMAUS ROAD

Dear Lord, the Emmaus road You walked
And found two souls, who sadly talked.
Then, as You approached them all alone,
It became quite clear You were unknown.
Their saddened, grieving, blinded sight
Could only focus on their own blight.
So as they spoke, they were confused
And He, at this point bemused,
Then opened up, His word to hear.
To bring to light and make it clear
That in their hearts was fear and doubt
But He was about to rout it out.
He spoke so clear and so profound
They begged Him stay and to expound.
And this He did, as He broke bread
So removing all their dread.
Their eyes were opened to the light
Just as their Lord vanished out of sight.

TROUGH THE VALLEY

On the path we take there be pit and snare,
But our dear Lord tells clearly to beware.
As through the valley of death and decay
The Spirit and word say, "Do not stay."
For comfort, they do promptly impart
And lead us quickly to depart.
Then as we obey the Master's voice,
He prepares a table of finest choice.
Our cup He fills to overflow
So with great rejoicing, on we go.

INTO HIS PRESENCE

Reverential fear should be our portion
As we are told, proceed with caution
Into the presence of our King.
What sacrifices do we bring?
Access, Holy Spirit, You do bestow
As through the blood, we surely go.
We should not forget the humble heart
Essential for the Master's part.
Holiness, the Lord has made most clear
For with it, there can be no fear.

LOVE'S QUEST

My Lord, my love, 'tis such a thrill
To know Your presence will instil
A confidence to calm and still
Such fears that try to claim my soul
For love's one quest, to make me whole.

HEALED

Lord Jesus, You are our healer
Having defeated our foe, the stealer.
Sweet Lord, You took the blessed position
To become our Great, our one physician.
Each stripe brought forth a glorious cure
T'was heavenly borne and totally sure.
As each lash bit into Your skin
We know our healing did begin.
Being redeemed from every attack
Having borne our scourging on Your back.

ALL IS WELL

The woman's heart just craved to give
Elisha's frame somewhere to live
Whilst on his travels, to and fro,
He'd surely have a place to go
Where he would find respite and care
And she would favour, with drink and fare.
Then with the thought and care He did perceive
Then spoke words of joy, she would conceive!
As years went by, her son did grow
Until one day, a tragic blow—
Her son was stricken and found dead.

The mother, to the prophet she fled
And when she finally reached his place
She sought to see him, face-to-face.
He did enquire of her son, do tell
With faith stirred up, said, "All is well."
Then with the woman, Elisha went
To find her son, whose life was spent?
Elisha embraced him, not once but twice
Then, praise God, just in a trice
He sneezed seven times, we are assured,
And opened his eyes, his life restored.
His mum, with rapturous joy, did expound
As she bowed her head upon the ground.

NAAMAN

The man was leprous, he needed healing.
He sought Elisha with such strong feeling.
This proved to be a prideful force
That left no room for humble course.
It caused his anger to omit
A precious truth he'd not admit.
The man of God was trying to deal
With this man's blight, which was quite real?
Presumptuous thoughts hindered progress
An offended soul made him regress.
He even questioned Elisha's request,
By questioning that he knew best.
Rage and arrogance was Naaman's statement
As he spurned God's word with resentment.
Then, praise God, as a humble soul,
He dipped seven times to be whole.
What joy behold, just to obey
Our Saviour's love goes all the way.

COMPELLING LOVE

My Lord, My King, You do constrain
As by Your side, I do remain.
Then as You walk and talk with me
I find such peace, I am set free
From every shackle that I once bore
Your precious love makes me quite sure.

UNSUPPRESSED JOY

Jesus, such love unfeigned
With us is still remaining.
T'is in this place of glee
A thrill to be with Thee.
How can my heart express
The joy of perfect mesh?
Quite rightly to impress
Such love you can't suppress.

IMMEASURABLE LOVE

Grateful I am that I am knit
Into Your love, not just a bit.
Such wondrous love to comprehend
Invades my heart as You do send
Such perfect love no height can reach
As I cry out and do beseech
To fathom a love that goes so deep
I must, I must, retain and keep
It is so precious, I'm satisfied
I stand amazed at just how wide
Your love, Your love, You do impart
And mightily bless my longing heart.

NO CONTEST

Whenever the enemy comes to town
Don't ever wear a worried frown
And do not let your soul go down
For he is but a toothless lion.
Since were adopted into Zion
This giant of fear is wind and puff
But we are filled with the real stuff.
So when we rise and do resist
He has no choice but to desist.

JESUS OUR PROVIDER

Jesus, our captain, strong and fair
Gives us armour that we must wear
Sends us out to face the trial
And gives us grace for every mile.
So when we use His word, our sword
We can rest in and be assured,
Victory is ours, Calvary secured.

FROM SNARE TO HEIR

A foolish disciple once said,
"I know the right road I must tread."
But pride and deceit was the bait
And the enemy just lay there, in wait.
These scurrilous traits drew him in
To a life that was peppered with sin.
But floundering, all help resisted
He went on his way, unassisted.
Then one day, he fell in the pit
Only to find it was dimly lit.
Then he cried out for help, and he leant
On his Saviour to truly repent.

And then, through God's mercy, he found

True love did greatly abound

That lifted him out of the mire

And gave him a place so much higher.

Such love, such wondrous love,

Our dear Saviour extends from above.

No matter, dear soul, what your blight

The sweet Lord will shed His pure light.

For the angels do truly rejoice

When the prodigal changes his voice

And then speaks words that thrill Father's ear

As he comes home again to be near.

———— ❧ ————

THE LIGHT

The light, the light, true light cascades
Into the earth, over hill and valley.
Such light, pure light, to souls invades
Then on its path removes all shades.
And as it draws all souls to rally
To be the light, He said, "Don't dally.
This radiance from us must shine
Till all who see it desire to be Mine."

BE STILL

Now when your life appears tranquil
Never neglect the call, be still:
For we have a foe who's never idle,
And given a chance, he's quite libel
To attack our minds and bring a doubt.
So immediately, we must cast him out
And "Know that I Am God" must be our shout.

AN EXPECTED DAY

Dear Lord, each morning when I wake
My soul cries out for me to make
This day's beginning a glorious start,
Which only comes as You Impart
Your wondrous mercy that's new each day.
So on my journey I will not stray
But to remain steadfast, I pray.
The day will then go as expected
Because You, dear Lord, will have protected.
Then as the day draws to a close,
I'll thank You Lord, no more impose
And then incline, in sweet repose.
My tired frame to You dispose.

LOVE'S CLEANSING FLOW

The blessings, Lord, of Your river flow
Continually from Your throne below.
Travelling with life-giving force
As it doth cleanse its charted course,
Allowing us divine discourse
So that our Lord can then impart
This cleansing flow into our heart.
And when the truth sinks deep within
We can proclaim we're free from sin.

NEVER THE SAME AGAIN

Lord, I come to You. This earthly frame
That's full of sin and racked with shame,
I lay it down at my Saviour's feet
And must confess, I am deplete.
Then You, sweet Lord, looked down on me
With such loving eyes and sympathy.
You then reached out, with love and peace
I can scarce believe—such blessed release.
My heart just leaped and was aglow
With such tender love that seemed to flow
Right through my being. I can't explain,
But I know I'll never be the same.

THE PRODIGAL

I looked, I searched, but could not find
A way of life that pleased my mind.
Earthly joy I sought, to my dismay,
As all it did was lead astray.
Pressing on, I would not surrender,
Selling my soul as a true offender.
Amid it all, the Lord did hear
An anguished cry from a heart of fear.
And I thank God, for the labourer found
Who did give all and did expound
The amazing grace that God has given
Through our precious Lord, whose side was riven.
So now, my Lord, my all I bring
To serve You always, my heavenly King.

THE LORD'S EMBRACE

Your presence, Lord, is such a blessing
Just as a mother's sweet caressing.
That gentle touch that finds its home
Within the heart that tends to roam.
The joy this brings, such pure delight,
Removing doubts right out of sight.
Your peace that truly does outstrip
The enemy's plans and wiles to grip.
Even the love in a mother's face
Cannot compare to our Lord's embrace.

UNITY [HE-ME SHE-THEE]

When he, and me, spend time with THEE
We find the key to life, so free.
When he, and me, are joined by she
It's clear the three is what should be.
In unity with THEE we three
Do reverently bow our knee.
It's how to be, for three, we see
Now when we three in THEE agree
This causes joyous glee to be
For we, free three, did not foresee
Such wondrous love stored up for we.

TEMPTATIONS

Temptations big, temptations small,
Whatever their size, we know that all
Are sent to try or to appall.
They are the wiles of a despised foe
We do perceive come from below.
So why then, do we oft time struggle
To take our stand, resisting trouble?
It seems to be that our remit
Is at the onset we don't submit
Our will and way to the Lord who cares,
For He's the one to foil the snares.
Then if we call on Jesus Christ,
It is His promise that in a tryst
To be our Rock, Strong Tower, and Strength,
Unflinching faith will be its length.
We overcome, victory secure
Our loving Saviour made this quite sure.

COMPASSION

When brother or sister need solace
It is our mission to frequent their place
With one intent— to bring God's love
And let it settle, just like a dove.
Sometimes a word or just a smile
Can carry the one an extra mile.
Then as compassion touches their heart
Their spirit is raised for a brand new start.
What joy it is, to serve this way
When we allow God's love the power to sway.

———————— ✿ ————————

GRACE

We gather together with one objective
To see our lives from God's perspective.
Sometimes it's good, sometimes disarming,
But with His love, 'tis never disarming
Because we know each truth revealed
Is better out than left concealed.
Then God does give a promise to share
And that is with His grace we'll bear.

HE KNOWS MY NAME

You know my name, You know my name,
Your word came forth, by three the same.
You brought me forth, from out the womb
And took me to Your secret room.
You showered me with many blessings
There is no room for any misgivings.
Your grace just lifts me to new heights
In which my heart truly delights.
Your word brings succour to my breast
And in Your love, I find Your rest.
You know my name, You know my name,
How so much more than worldly fame!
The world promotes a tarnished image
Its influence to form a visage
Of how mankind must seek approval
By hardening hearts and love's removal.
But we thank You for our salvation
As we're adopted into Your nation.
And through the garden, You know my name,
Through Calvary's pain, You know my name,
Such wondrous love was not in vain
For You, Dear Lord, DO KNOW MY NAME.

GOD'S HEIR

I AM, I AM, the great I AM,
The one who spoke with Abraham,
Through whom my Jesus is the seed,
And faith in Christ fulfils my need.
This mystery shows such tender concern
For the great I AM makes us His heirs.
So why did God bestow such gifts?
For to contemplate this truth just lifts
My heart, my soul to a whole new sphere
And completely removes all trace of fear.
Now His word makes abundantly clear,
I, as His child, must draw near
To represent my great High King

As an ambassador of the heavenly thing
That He expects from His heirs of grace.
As we with patience run the race
We can be sure for He has said
If in obedience the path we tread
Causes us to savour the one true bread
Then we fulfil His will and plan
And will find favour with God and man.
Then as I make this authority mine
As your own child I will shine
And bring to a needful world that's carnal
An Agape love that's quite supernal.

FERVENT PRAYER

As we kneel in fervent prayer,
Concealed away from worldly glare
In our holy, secret closet
Ready, our prayers to deposit.
The joy it brings, just to relate
Our heart's deep longings, without debate.
To know our Lord hears every word
Seems to the world a thing absurd.
But not to us, His chosen ones.
Because we're free, from worldly bonds.
We are transported to this heavenly place
As we kneel and seek His face.

GOD'S THOUGHT

What privilege to share with those
The joy of knowing, what sweet repose
Your presence with me does impose.
One fleeting, passing, precious thought
Is gleamed important to be brought
Into my mind, so I may see
What precious truth You have for me.
From this blessing will surely flow
As You, dear Lord, want me to know,
And grasp this nugget of gold divine
To then embrace and make it mine.

TRUE FELLOWSHIP

Dear Lord, how do we explain
The joy of Your sweet refrain?
When in Your presence, we do wait
To enjoy Your tender touch.
To us, that means oh, so much.
Whatever our condition
We assume our position,
As on our knees or on our face
We know this is our rightful place
To fellowship, our heart's appeal
With Him who died and made it real.

LOVE'S LONGING

My heart longs and deeply pines
To spend precious moments with love divine.
My heart leaps at the sound of Your voice—
What a privilege to make this my choice!
And for us to meet in this special place
Enriches my life with such pure grace,
Excites my soul, the thought of meeting
My risen Lord and cherish His greeting:
"My son, come now, let Me love and embrace.
I've longed for you to seek My face."

ON WHOM DO YOU LEAN?

When life seems hard and very mean
It's good to know on whom we lean.
But if you doubt just who is there,
Get on your knees, and spare
A moment in a busy day
To seek the Lord, the only way.
And as you lay your life to bare,
He'll show Himself as one to care.
So as your confidence in Him is seen,
You'll then be sure on whom you lean.

———— ✥ ————

IT IS MINE

Sweet Jesus, when You bore my sin,
Such precious love just drew me in.
You then poured out Your grace divine
That was sent by love divine
And crowned it all and made it mine.

OUR CHOICE

The eagle flies to heights unseen
Where other birds have never been.
The chicken never leaves earth's crust
And oft is found scratching dust.
The eagle sees a storm is coming
And with such power, is overcoming.
The chicken, with head pressed down,
If only could, would wear a frown.
The eagle's view is pure azure
The chicken, well, is never sure.
The one delights in God's creation
The other fears a chef's imagination.
Now we've been given God's resources,
So let us soar to His planned courses.
For our desire MUST be the eagle's quest,
For to be a chicken is not God's best.

JOB DONE

If life deals you a serious blow,
Whether health, or finance—you never know—
Don't run about like a headless chicken
Because in a whirl, you're easy picking
For the toothless lion that's on the prowl
Seeking whom he may devour.
But slap him down and make him howl
For our precious Lord victory has won,
On Calvary, the job was done.

SEEK FIRST

Your word says, "Seek My Kingdom first,
And righteousness should be your thirst."
So with this thought so firmly planted,
It makes pure sense to not supplant it
With anything that would detract
From God's profound and precious fact.

HOLINESS

Dear Lord, to Holiness You have called
All Your children; to be enthralled
In Your purity, to see You, Lord.
So we will all be quite assured
That as we yield ourselves to Thee,
We will enjoy Your company.
As at Your table, we will serve,
Bringing the sacrifice You deserve.

PRESS ON

Your word says, Lord, that we must press
Continually on through Satan's mess.
And even more, You do impress,
For us to gain complete redress,
We must pursue and harass our foe.
We don't have time to wail and woe.
This is the battle to which we're called,
So don't allow ourselves to be stalled
For victories ours, this is recalled.

NARROW WAY

As I travel God's narrow course,
I find no reason for remorse
Because the one right by my side
Is my blessed Lord, who bore my pride.
Then as I cherish such rich discourse,
He gently reveals He is my source.
And as He answers my fervent prayer,
I find such peace, for my Lord does care.
What assurance this gives to share
For now I know, He's always there.

DROWNING MAN

Holy Spirit, revealer of mysteries sought,
You fill our hearts with wondrous thoughts.
And as we seek to embrace these facts,
Tender love steps in and promptly acts
To do the thing He surely can
To save the sinful, drowning man.

ALONE WITH JESUS

It is such joy to be set free
To fellowship alone with Thee.
For precious, intimate, pure discourse
Can only be found with You, the source.
You are the font of all our needs
And You expound Your heavenly creeds.
Because of this, I do desire
To spend more time, as You require,
And grow, and grow, in Your pure light
To live the life and do what's right.

JESUS IS CAPTAIN

As we seek to walk in grace,
The Holy Spirit never forces the pace,
But gently quickens our longing soul
Toward the place to be made whole.
Though the path can have its snare,
We can be sure that He is there.
As He navigates around despair,
His mercy helps us stay afloat
For Jesus is captain of our boat.

THE VISTA

As the sun peeped over the trees
And I felt the gentle breeze,
The mirrored image upon the lake
Reflected Gods glory which is never fake
To enjoy this vista is a heavenly sight,
But to walk God's path is pure delight.
To see God's Son, having been raised high,
To feel God's presence brings a gasping sigh.
And in God's image, we are sure
For it's not of man, God made us pure.
So as we seek God's kingdom first,
This vista is what makes us thirst.

PEACE

JEHOVAH SHALOM is our sweet Lord
And transcends understanding, even when aboard.
For this fruit brings sweet release
So we can rest in His perfect peace.

JONAH

A man was called from out his zone
With a special message, straight from the throne.
It was to go to a certain city
For which the Lord grieved with pity.
However, the man chose to disobey
And promptly went the opposite way.
He boarded a boat to make an escape
Which proved to be a great mistake.
It wasn't long till the boat got battered

So to prevent the crew from being scattered,
They cast the man into the deep
And then found calm so they could sleep.
It was quite clear that the man did fail
But to finally end inside a whale
(Even for him was beyond the pale).
So he cried out to repent
And sought the Lord; might He relent?
God then enforced His previous plan
And demanded obedience from the man.
The message was quite plain and clear,
If only they would heed and hear.
It was to deliver them from themselves
If only their own ways, they would shelve.
The city repented without delay,
Allowing God's compassion to have its sway.
The moral here is very plain:
If you want to avoid needless pain,
Obey at once, all else is vain.

TRUST AND OBEY

I never know where the Spirit will lead,
But one thing is sure—He'll meet my need.
Whether a time, or place, or a man,
I know that I know that the Spirit can
Bring about my Saviour's wonderful plan.
And when I trust Him and obey,
My conviction must be that I will stay
Firmly grafted to love divine
So all His promises will be mine.

OUR ARMOUR

We have armour that fits our frame
Divinely tailored by our Lord, the same.
Each piece fits snugly, like a glove
We can be sure it's from above.
This suit must never be discarded
But 24/7 should be regarded.
To omit one piece is to misguide
Lest the enemy would soon deride.
Now whilst each piece is in its place,
The enemy can't see your face.
As far as he knows, it is the Lord.
So with his discernment severely flawed,
We claim our victory, he's overawed.

ESTHER

Queen Esther was the king's delight.

And the king's approval gave her the right

To bring concerns and state her blight

So seated, at the dining table.

At the king's request, she was able

To bring her care to the one who should

Reverse the plans, as only he could.

And in the presence of Esther's foe

The king decreed the way to go.

So that same day, her foe was vanquished

And Esther's cares were completely banished.

Now we, as children of the Lord Most High,

Have a greater advocate to meet our sigh.

For Calvary was our Saviour's pleasure

To meet our needs beyond all measure.

THE STORM RAGES

The storm raged, fear to instil,
Our Lord looked and said, "Peace— be still."
The storm calmed, Jesus had spoken.
His strong faith remained unbroken.
When we experience flickering doubt,
Don't be afraid—to the Lord, call out.
He's always there; His promise is sure.
Jesus is just waiting for the open door,
He then will calm the troubled heart
And lead you to a place apart
Where you'll find peace, which does transcend
Our understanding right to the end.

DAVID AND GOLIATH

Now the Lord said to Samuel, "Just go
To the house of Jesse, for to show
My way, my will, in this thing,
You will anoint young David as king."
One day, Jesse sent David out and said,
"Go down to your brothers with this bread."
But as David went down to the war,
He couldn't believe just what he saw.
All the men were frightened and fearful,
Being daily subjected to a blasphemous earful
Of threats and abuse from this Philistine infidel.
David determined his tongue must be stilled
As the lion and bear, he would be killed.
Then scorned and rejected,

But never dejected,

He kept pressing his case to the king

That his only need was his sling.

Then finally, allowed to go,

He prepared to put on a show.

For he rejected the taunts of the giant

And with sling and stones quite defiant,

He stood his ground, so assured.

Proclaiming with the giant's own sword,

In the power of his wonderful Lord,

His head would be removed from his torso

To confidently show, even more so,

That to defy the Lord God of Hosts

With all his empty boasts

Would only bring death and defeat

As he falls at the Master's feet.

MY REST

When Jesus opens another door,
We may not know just what's in store.
But if we alight from our comfort boat
And look to Jesus, He'll keep us afloat.
Then as He leads with such divinity,
We'll meet new friends and enjoy affinity.
Our communion with all will be so blessed
For in this place is perfect rest.

RIGHTEOUSNESS

Why does our Lord impart this thing?
It surely is so He can bring
Us to ourselves, free from pride
So we can walk right by His side.
Then as we seek first this precious gift,
It will dispel all fear of rift
From God, the one who sent it down,
Imputing us with His heavenly crown,
Enabling us to walk and reign
As we receive this essential gain.
This also brings us into grace
So we may walk at our Lord's pace,
Looking to a life that is eternal
And knowing it to be quite supernal.

THE FIERY TRIAL

They cast three men into the fire,
Expecting to see their lives expire.
But as the King looked, he became confused
And then became greatly mused.
The King exclaimed to his aides, "Look, then,
Am I not seeing, in the fire, four men?
This fourth man is as a god, I see.
How can they possibly be walking free?
I will call them out and will decree
That all will worship their God with me."

GOD FIRST

As God's own children, we follow His word
To do any other would be quite absurd.
We witness to others of our loving Saviour,
Encouraging them He should be their savour.
Then to expound, with great delight,
The wonders of His glorious light,
For then their eyes gain spiritual sight
As they seek first all that is right.
Then onward and upward they do rise,
(Which, when considered, is no surprise).
To the Lord's promises they do cling
And through obedience, they do bring
Their lives as a living sacrifice
Knowing nothing else will suffice.

WHY THE CRY

Lord, You insisted, "Go to the other side."
T'was not a choice, but clear directive
So to obey would bring no chide.
And then with Him, we will abide.
So to fulfil the divine objective,
His word must never be rejected.
Then, why the cry, "Lord, don't You care?"
Would sadden His heart and cause despair.
Now Lord, we know we're not forsaken
Therefore our faith should not be shaken.
For as Your love casts out all fear,
Your amazing Grace draws us so near.

MAKE IT THROUGH

When life throws a vicious curve,
It's so easy to lose our nerve.
And because our plans do go astray,
We must never allow ourselves to sway.
For if our thoughts go to dismay,
We'll lose our focus on love's right way.
Then this will cause our hearts to pine
And we'll lose sight of love Divine
For separation from our dear Lord,
Even for a moment, should be deplored.
We must see the attack, for what's intended
To bring us low, if not contended.
But we know better, the word is true
And with God's help, we'll make it through.

FEAR NOT

Fear not, fear not, my precious heir,
I am Your God, and I do care.
Deep breath, deep breath, and wait for me
Have I not promised eternity
To those who trust and obey My call?
My angels will not let you fall.
They'll bear you up on wings of hope
And teach you always how to cope.

THE LIGHT

Lord Jesus, Your light shines oh, so bright
That nothing can keep it from our sight.
It reaches the darkest depths of man
Then illuminates God's precious plan.

TRUST GOD

Sometimes, Dear Lord, as storms prevail
I thank my God He does not fail.
For as I'm tempted for Satan's wiles to consider,
My precious Lord is there to deliver.
As traps and snares try to draw me in,
My comfort, My Lord, delivers from sin.
The gallows were raised to destroy
But God did reverse and did employ
Its use to remove the enemy's ploy.
Now the pit has been our abode on occasion,
But our sweet Lord has no limitation
And lifts us out, with much jubilation.
So now, Holy Spirit, as the descending dove
How can I not trust in Your amazing love?

REJOICE

Lord Jesus, our high Priest and King,
We humbly bow to You and bring
Our living sacrifice and praise
And then rejoice, as You do raise.
Our earthly frame to be beside
You Lord Jesus to reside

OUR INVESTITURE

My Lord, my King, I do draw near
To kneel before in reverent fear.
You summon me to enter in
To give my all, new life to bring.
Your Majesty, it is with glee
You allow me bend a humble knee.

And in Your presence—what pure delight!
Just knowing, my King, we're in Your sight,
But that's not all—why, we've been called!
For with great joy, You have installed
Each one of us a new position
And with Your help, a heavenly mission.
With head bowed down, before my Lord,
You touch my frame with Your own sword
To ratify and to appoint
And send us forth, as You anoint
Us into battle, armed with Your power
Ensuring us You're our strong tower.
But more, much more, You do invest
As we proceed to do our best.
Ambassadors, we now are known
Confessing words straight from the throne.
Authority over all is given
As by Your love, we're truly driven.
To seal it all, as only You could,
Our Lord and Saviour, shed Your blood.

GOD'S SWORD

Press on! Press on! "Against what?" I ask,
Hidden forces, the foe is your task.
So, how do I conquer a hidden force?
With weapons supplied by God, of course.
Then, what are the weapons I use to fight?
The sword of the Spirit is first by right.
With this, the Lord releases His might.
So how do I obtain this powerful sword?
Well, first you must be of one accord
With God's own word, which is His sword.
The Spirit will show you how to wield
This trusty weapon and with His shield,
You'll stand quite firm and be not moved
For God's weaponry cannot be improved.

OUR PROVIDER

When we walk with the Lord, we're correctly attired
So when we're attacked, we won't get tired.
You see our protection is totally inclusive
And is for whosoever—never exclusive.
The Lord knows our need to be on our guard
For the enemy attacks right in our back yard.
He's not selective; he'll strike where he can
For he totally relies on the ignorance of man.
But God is so good, His promises sure.
He gave us His spirit, so loving and pure,
So as we embrace Jehovah Jireh
We're fully assured He is our provider.

GOD IN ALL

God's so good, creation rejoice!
As spring breaks forth to tend its course
The lambs are born and leap with glee
As in the meadow they do run free.
The ducklings, furiously paddle to keep
Abreast of mum, as they do reap
The titbits, which the children do throw,
All of which does help them grow.
The busy hen, her fledglings fed,
Tendered their needs, made ready for bed.
And as the long day draws to a close,
There's such a peace, in sweet repose.
Our feathered friends, a chorus bring
In perfect unison they do sing.
A beautiful day, I do recall
And I do thank God, for being our ALL.

GOD'S PACE

The gentle flowing stream
Just brings a peace serene
The mighty rushing river
Can cause our spines to shiver
One leads me to a tranquil place
The other fires my thoughts at pace
One speaks of life and quiet order
The other of rush and intense fervour
They both do speak of life's encounters
But our dear Lord is our surmounter

It matters not what the condition
We are assured that the Lord's petition
Is being made at the throne of grace
So we can walk at God's own pace
Securing victory in our earthly race

PERSONIFIED LOVE

Dear Father God, in Your time and season
You invaded earth's mess for this sole reason:
To send an angel to the Virgin Mary
(Which for her must have been quite scary.)
To tell her a child she would conceive,
A thing she found hard to believe
Seeing that she had never known a man
But the angel insisted, "With God, you can!"
So the Holy Spirit touched Mary's condition
And nine months later there was fruition;
However, this fruit was God's vine incarnate
To foil Satan's plan and to frustrate
By redeeming mankind to its original state
And disposing of sin through His precious blood.
Bought by our Saviour as only He could,
What amazing love Jesus did decree
As He hung alone on Calvary's tree.

STRESS

Now stress is an enemy of our soul
And robs the saint of being made whole.
We need to face the facts of life
For stress is used to bring us strife.
But if we adopt our rightful stance
Our enemy simply has no chance.
He can't afflict a soul this way
If we stand firm and do not sway.
For with the power invested in us,
We turn the table on him because
He has no authority to touch our mind.
And this is confirmed in the word we find,
For our testimony of Grace released
And supported by His blood increased
Gives us the victory to overcome
And this for all and not just some.

THE FOUR ARKS

Father God, you did set old Noah a task
And praise you, Lord, he didn't question or ask.
But at Your instructions, he proceeded to build
A boat right there in the middle of a field.
You called it an ark, or chest to contain
The people and animals You would maintain.
This protected Your righteousness, if just for a season,
And history shows You had a good reason.
For later, He spoke to Moses His man
And blessed him by sharing Your next mighty plan.
You told him to build an ark for Your dwelling,
Instructing all the need to face their failing.

All this, of course, was a foretaste of grace,
Which we now know flows from only one place.
Then Jesus appeared, the True Ark and Saviour,
Within was contained the sweet smelling savour
Of Your heavenly riches, so abundantly given.
When on Calvary's cross His side was riven,
Lord God, in completion, Jesus ascended
Back to His home, from whence He descended.
The reason for this expedient act
Was to send the Spirit, a wonderful fact,
To live in us, a divine mark
And seal His saints as His final ARK.

EMOTIONS

Emotions come, emotions go.

And when they're present, others know.

Some are good, others bad.

One makes us happy, others sad.

Some last a while, some very quick,

And how we deal is not a trick.

For this I know they're not selective

In fact, we're all open and very receptive,

So don't be alarmed that they're most subjective.

Learn to deal and be objective.

Now the emotions, no matter how real,

Should never be allowed for a second to steal

The peace and balance our Lord gives

To the inner man that thrives and lives

To be completely led by the Holy Spirit.

So control the emotions as would befit

A child of God, it's our remit.

JEHOVAH JIREH

Jehovah Jireh, a redemptive title
That allows His children and does entitle
Them to bring their cares to the throne of Grace
And then to leave them in that place.
For this is where the Lord's provision
Is perfectly metered and needs no revision.
Then we relax in sweet recline
Knowing, with Jesus, all is fine.

REDEEMED

I am redeemed by the blood of the Lamb,
Now I stand firm with the great I AM.
So, victory He has now made sure
To His child through love so pure.
He then bestows His amazing grace
For His disciples to run the race.

HE LEADS ME

Dear Lord, You lead me by the hand
Into the new and promised land,
Wherein I'm taught the joy of living
From a heart of love that is ever-giving.
You've opened up to me, it's true,
A blessed walk that is brand new.
And on that path, sometimes quite tough,
I am assured, You are enough.
And as my path goes through the valley,
Your still small voice says, "Don't dwell or dally."
So onward, upward I will climb
To where I find Love's Love, sublime.
Therein, I find rest and grace
As I look into Jesus' face.

THE CROSS

Sweet Lord Jesus, You died for me.
As by those nails, You hung on the tree.
You bowed Your head that bore the thorns
And then forgave all the scorns.
Your body limp and wracked with pain,
Gave up the ghost so we could reign.
Then by Your side a soldier did peer
Into Your face as he thrust his spear
To fulfil the Father's will.
You did allow Your blood to spill
So from that moment and forever
We trust the blood, not our endeavour.

OUR ANCHOR

Through test and trial, Love knows our pain.
He comforts us, so we remain
Steadfast and sure. The anchor casts
Out in the deep to make us fast.
This precious hope that quells the soul
As in His presence, we are made whole.

BEAUTIFUL VIEW

Lord, as I share my heart with You,
You open up a marvellous view.
Into the depths, as yet unseen,
Of Your pure word that makes me clean.
As then the Spirit controls my thoughts,
My mind transcends to Your inner courts.

Therein your beauty is revealed,
In wondrous light, till now concealed.

SWEET LOVE

Sweet love poured out to rend the veil
To meet Love's blood, shed through travail
To give us access to the throne
So we should never walk alone.

AT THE THRONE

What privilege! To enter in
Cleansed by the blood from the stain of sin.
It goes beyond our highest prayer
When with the Master, we sit and share.

ASSURANCE

What sheer delight, assurance gained
When with sweet Jesus, we rule and reign.
It was for us He gave His all,
So we should never have to fall.

———— ✿ ————

ENTHRALLING LOVE

Sweet love descended to my heart
So I would be set apart
To serve my King, to give my all,
And rest in peace, His love enthral.

THE LORD'S BATTLE

What wondrous solace and pure delight
When our enemy is put to flight
Not by our strength, as we perceive,
But by love's grace that we receive.

HOLY SPIRIT

Holy Spirit, You are mine
Being sent by Love divine
To reveal from deep within
The true Love that cleanses sin.

Holy Spirit, strong and true
Lead me to the pastures new,
Quicken me with pure delight
As You lift me in God's sight.

Holy Spirit, God's precious choice,
I welcome You, that still small voice.
When my heart just yearns to hear
The sweet comfort that You are near.

Holy Spirit, pure river of love
Released by our Saviour's precious blood
Heals the hurt of a damaged soul
Brings Love's peace, as yet untold.

Such wondrous love
Such wondrous love
My Saviour gives to me.
Such wondrous love
Such wondrous love
Forever let it be.

Selah (Pause and calmly think of that)

SPIRIT OF LOVE

Spirit of Love, never let me go
For in Your presence, I must grow.
And as Your love flows through my heart,
I am greatly assured You will never depart.

Spirit of Love, please let it be
A continuous river of blessing to me.
Your wondrous love, so strong and true
Enfolds and soaks me with Your dew.

Spirit of Love, You search the thing
Within my heart that I must bring
Into Your presence. I yield and fall
To allow Your love to consume it all.

Spirit of Love, so very tender
I give my all in full surrender:
My soul, my heart, my will, I trust
For in sweet love, I surely must.

Spirit of Love, You fill my heart
With such deep love, I will not depart.
For the amazing taste of Love divine
Compels my heart to a joy sublime.

SON OF LOVE

Son of Love, You sank so deep
To enter into the enemy's keep.
Therein to retrieve that which was taken
Such love, pure love, cannot be shaken.

Son of Love, precious fruit divine,
Laid down Your life to make it mine.
Gave up the ghost for the seed to sow,
And in the blood Your love will grow.

Son of Love, to You I yield
For You are my strength and shield.
I cling to You as my solid rock
And bid farewell to all who mock.

Son of Love, for this came down:
To bestow on us a heavenly crown,
To make each one a royal priest
From the greatest to the least.

Son of Love, You raised the dead
And then gave us this precious bread.
For now, oh, precious Love, You crave
To see Your children, strong and brave.

Son of Love, deity laid down,
You came to save without a frown.
Forgiven all to set men free
And give us a legacy.

Son of Love, forever ours
For entering into endless hours
You took upon the sin of all
So we're complete and cleansed from all.

Son of Love, most precious gift
Sent from the throne to heal the rift,
To give back Eden's priceless store
To reconcile and to restore.

Son of Love, God's wondrous grace,
Gave Your all and so replaced
The prideful sin that so beset
With precious love that broke the net.

Son of Love, who walked on sea
Then calmed the storm that I might see.
Said, "Come", to me and, "Be set free
From fear and walk the walk with Me."

Son of Love, as they were scourging
Your loving thought was for our purging
And as the lashes cut Your flesh
Your love for us made perfect mesh.

Son of Love, to hell you went
To meet with those whose lives were spent.
And through such love that is not bound
You reached the souls of all You found.

Son of Love, You did disarm
The enemy that gave alarm
By nailing all to Your rugged cross
And cleansing souls of sin and dross.

Son of Love, in glory raised
To take your seat and to be praised,
To minister in the Holy Place,
Where we behold Your wondrous grace.

Son of Love, Love shed abroad
You draw me to You, sweet Lord.
And in that place of peace and rest,
My heart cries out, You are the best!

Son of Love, no one like You,
You are supreme in all You do.
Your endless love You don't withhold
When You succour to meek and bold.

Son of Love, with fish and bread
You fed all those to You were led
Then healed the multitudes of pain
And preached the word for certain gain.

Son of Love, You raised a man
From death, the grave, and Satan's plan
Then his friends, for all to see,
Had his grave clothes loosed—set free.

Son of Love, love's love divine
Holds my heart in sweet recline.
Takes my soul to perfect rest,
Strengthens me, for all is blessed

Son of Love, You are my friend
And on You I do depend.
As a branch fixed to Your love,
I'll bear fruit from heaven above.

Son of Love, You've called me out
And cleansed me from all fear and doubt.
I'm lifted up to the throne of grace
Where I find warmth in Your sweet embrace.

Son of Love, unfeigned You be
That You should pour such love on me.
I scarce can grasp the enormity
Of love's wondrous Calvary.

Son of Love, God's one true vine,
Resplendent in love's fruit divine
Enthrals my soul with such great pleasure
Then blessed me beyond all measure.

Son of Love, divine made man,
Transcends our thoughts to God's own plan,
Opens our eyes to His glorious light
Then keeps us in His attentive sight.

Son of Love, God's heart revealed
Shows us the things that He repealed
That I might taste and see what's good,
So that the seed would be made bud.

Son of Love, Your blessings flow
To Your dear children here below.
Your blessings, which do overtake,
Compelled to love, for love's pure sake.

Son of Love, You sought my heart
And with compassion, you impart
A glorious life with You to share,
Crowned always with the love I bear.

Son of Love, such pure delight
You fill my heart with heavenly light.
And Your fire burns deep within,
Which can't be quenched by worldly sin.

Son of Love, in me You reign.
From deep within, it is made plain
That from the fountain of Your love
Your name is lifted high above.

Son of Love, You found my pit
And through Your love, You entered it.
There is no place that You won't go
To shed Your love and heavenly glow.

Son of Love, to man You came
To sacrifice Your precious frame.
With outstretched arms, You bared your soul
So all alike will be made whole.

Son of Love, in Gethsemane
Your heart opened wide to what must be.
Pure drops of blood flowed from your brow
As Your pure love just showed us how.

Son of Love, what discernment You brought
You even know our every thought.
The truth of this is most profound
And we thank Love, You do expound.

Son of Love, our Great High Priest and King
You've endowed us with Your heavenly ring:
The precious gift of reconciliation
To lead others to Your salvation.

Son of Love, You give increase
To all of those who seek Your peace.
What beauty, what worth there is in growth
To the ones that are betrothed.

Son of Love, seated on high
We long to see You, by and by.
And You will come to us again
To raise us up with You to reign.

Son of Love, hung so forlorn
Yet from Your visage, a new birth born.
And from Your side, the crimson flood
Now we have victory through Your blood.

Son of Love, led by the Spirit
Made plain the path so we'd not miss it.
Explained the truth of God's own will
Then gave Your grace so we'd fulfil.

Son of Love, You took our pain
So we have no reason to complain.
You came to earth, our heavenly King,
And so You made us Your offspring.

Son of Love, You put to flight
Our enemies' plan, clear from our sight.
You raised Your standard, oh, so high,
So we'd find comfort by and by.

Son of Love, Your banner be
An assuring comfort and guard to me.
And as I rest in love's respite,
I gain an inner, powerful might.

Son of Love, to Your house You draw
Through what is mine, the open door.
You wave Your banner, which is love,
Then pour blessing from above.

Son of Love, victory is mine
As at Your table we do recline.
Our triumph is a precious gain
When all is done in Jesus' name.

Son of Love, we wrestle not
With evil men who plan and plot.
But with Your overcoming power
We call on You, our mighty tower.

———— ⚬ ————

about the
AUTHOR

I was born in England in 1944, and for most of my life I lived in a city called Leicester. Leicester sheep were abundant, and the predominant industry of the area was hosiery manufactures, so this made me what was locally called "a woolly back." Most of the wool used was obtained from local farmers, and on a visit to Williamsburg in Virginia many years later, I found it amazing that Leicester sheep had found their way to America.

I have been married for almost 50 years. My wife and I have one daughter, who is married to an American and has lived in America for eight years. We have a 5-year-old granddaughter who keeps us fit and exhausted, and we wouldn't have it any other way — or so my wife tells me.

We are a Christian family. My wife and I gave our hearts to the Lord in 1984 on March 28 at 11 p.m. Our walk with the Lord has had uncounted valleys and mountains; however, we can truthfully say that He has always been there with us. His love has been displayed in the most astounding ways, not least since we came to live in America in May 2015, being led by Him to Joy Church in Matthews, N.C.

Over the years, my employment has varied from managerial positions in the manufacturing sector to law enforcement as a prison officer, none of which led me to ever consider becoming a poet. But, the Lord had a different plan, and so you now hold my book in your hands.

This is the first book I have ever written. It is totally by the inspiration of the Holy Spirit, who literally woke me up in the early hours of the morning, back in late February 2015, and gave me the first poem. That encounter proved to be the first of many wonderful visits that I consider very precious to me.

www.ingramcontent.com/pod-product-compliance
Lightning Source LLC
LaVergne TN
LVHW021549080426
835510LV00019B/2450